Copyright © 2019 by Jennifer King

All rights reserved. No part of this publication may be reproduced, distributed, or transmitted in any form or by any means, including photocopying, recording, or other electronic or mechanical methods, without the prior written permission of the publisher, except in the case of brief quotations embodied in critical reviews and certain other noncommercial uses permitted by copyright law. For permission requests, write to the publisher at: jai@jaipublishing.com

Ordering Information: Quantity sales. Special discounts are available on quantity purchases by corporations, associations, and others. For details, contact the publisher at the electronic address above.

Printed in the United States of America

ISBN-13: 9781097941377

Get your FREE Chains Checklist at www.33yearsaslave.com

COMPANION JOURNAL

~~33~~ 12 YEARS A

Removing the chains from life, love & business

JENNIFER KING

Get your FREE Chains Checklist at www.33yearsaslave.com

HOW TO USE THIS JOURNAL

Welcome to Your *33 Years A Slave*

33-Day Journal

It is important that YOU identify what chains are holding YOU back in life. Often times we are so busy living life that we don't realize that we have collected so many chains.

In order to get the most out of this journal, don't try to complete it all at once. Instead, EACH day take ONE chain, and as you go throughout your day, be MINDFUL of what you could have if that chain was removed.

Think about where the chain came from and why the chain has so much power over you. More importantly, think about how you can get help to get the chain removed.

When you realize JUST how much these chains are holding you back, then it is quite possible that you will be willing to do whatever it takes to get them taken off.

So that you can claim the Freedom that has been yours all along.

Sending you Love and Hope for this Journey...

Jennifer King

Slave No More

Get your FREE Chains Checklist at www.33yearsaslave.com

DAY 1
Chains of Fear

Everyone is afraid of something. Fear is quite human; however, failure to act because of our fear is what holds us back. As you go about your day today, think about how fear is keeping you from living your best life, and resign to get help to either remove the fear, or at least learn how to not allow it to render you ineffective.

What am I MOST afraid of?

_____

_____

_____

_____

_____

Where did this fear come from?

_____

_____

_____

_____

What is this fear costing me?

_____

_____

_____

_____

What is my plan to move forward?

_____

_____

_____

_____

Get your FREE Chains Checklist at www.33yearsaslave.com

DAY 2

Chains of Comfort & Complacency

It's amazing how we can trick ourselves into being comfortable EVEN in the worst situations. Job's we hate, marriages that were over long ago, you get the picture. In what areas have you been settling with what you have instead of seeking more?

_____
_____
_____
_____

In what area(s) of my life am I MOST comfortable and complacent?

_____
_____
_____
_____

Get your FREE Chains Checklist at www.33yearsaslave.com

Where did this comfort and complacency come from?

_____

_____

_____

_____

_____

_____

What is it costing me to be so comfortable and complacent?

_____

_____

_____

_____

_____

_____

Get your FREE Chains Checklist at www.33yearsaslave.com

DAY 3
Chains of Checks

What checklist am I keeping in my life?

_____
_____
_____
_____
_____

Where did this checklist come from?

_____
_____
_____

What is it costing me to keep this checklist in my life?

Get your FREE Chains Checklist at www.33yearsaslave.com

DAY 4
Chains of Legacy

Our parents used to say, "Do what I say, not what I do", but we can't help but replicate what we see growing up. Whether it's hard work, poverty, abusive relationships, etc., we tend to mimic what we see and carry it with us all of our lives.

What Chains of Legacy am I wearing?

_____

_____

_____

_____

_____

_____

Where did these Chains of Legacy come from?

_____

_____

_____

_____

_____

What is it costing me to keep these Chains of Legacy in my life?

_____

_____

_____

_____

_____

Get your FREE Chains Checklist at www.33yearsaslave.com

DAY 5
Other People's Chains

Oftentimes, we are influenced by other people's opinions of us, our lifestyle, our choices, etc. And sometimes, we allow their insecurities to spill over into what we are doing, thus taking on their chains as our own.

What chains am I wearing from other people?

_____
_____
_____
_____
_____
_____

Get your FREE Chains Checklist at www.33yearsaslave.com

Where/who did these chains come from?

_____
_____
_____
_____
_____
_____

What is it costing me to keep these chains in my life?

_____
_____
_____
_____
_____
_____

Get your FREE Chains Checklist at www.33yearsaslave.com

DAY 6
The Chains of Jobs

There are very few among us who were NOT told to get a good job and retire… But what happens when jobs change, and the world changes? What's next? No one told us that, which is why many of us have been left to rot in the corporate cubicles of jobs.

What Chains of Jobs am I wearing?

_____

_____

_____

_____

_____

_____

Where did these Chains of Jobs come from?

_____
_____
_____
_____
_____
_____

What is it costing me to continue to wear these Chains of Jobs?

_____
_____
_____
_____
_____
_____

Get your FREE Chains Checklist at www.33yearsaslave.com

DAY 7
The Chains of Hard Work

Today, we live in a world where intellect and thinking outside of the box will get you MUCH further than HARD WORK. Those who work HARD, make the least. We have replaced creative thinking with hard work, thinking it will get us where we need to go.

What Chains of Hard work am I wearing?

_____

_____

_____

_____

_____

_____

Get your FREE Chains Checklist at www.33yearsaslave.com

Where did these chains of Hard work come from?

_____

_____

_____

_____

_____

_____

What is it costing me to continue to wear these Chains of Hard work?

_____

_____

_____

_____

_____

_____

Get your FREE Chains Checklist at www.33yearsaslave.com

DAY 8

The Chains of Education

Go to school and get a good job was told to me over and over again. We hear it from society, teachers, administrators, employers, television shows, etc. It's all around us. This message that if we get an education, we can get a good paying job.

What Chains of Education am I wearing?

_____

_____

_____

_____

_____

_____

Where did these Chains of Education come from?

_____
_____
_____
_____
_____
_____

What is it costing me to continue to wear these Chains of Education?

_____
_____
_____
_____
_____
_____

Get your FREE Chains Checklist at www.33yearsaslave.com

DAY 9

The Chains of Money

Along with more money comes more responsibilities. Also, along with money comes accountability. If you can't be responsible or accountable to the money you are making, you risk losing it all.

What Chains of Money am I wearing?

_____
_____
_____
_____
_____

Where did these Chains of Money come from?

_____

_____

_____

_____

_____

_____

What is it costing me to continue to wear these Chains of Money?

_____

_____

_____

_____

_____

_____

Get your FREE Chains Checklist at www.33yearsaslave.com

DAY 10

The Chains of Love

Getting caught up in an intimate relationship, losing yourself in the process, benefits no one, especially that relationship. Checking off the marriage box was an accomplishment that I didn't fully understand. I ended up ignoring the warning signs just so I could check off the box.

What Chains of Love am I wearing?

_____

_____

_____

_____

_____

_____

Where did these Chains of Love come from?

___

___

___

___

___

___

What is it costing me to continue to wear these Chains of Love?

___

___

___

___

___

___

Get your FREE Chains Checklist at www.33yearsaslave.com

DAY 11

The Chains of Unhappiness

No way I would tell anyone that I was truly unhappy. I held that secret inside for so long. The weight of the unhappiness wore me down physically, mentally and spiritually. Until I could no longer keep that secret.

What Chains of Unhappiness am I wearing?

_____

_____

_____

_____

_____

_____

Get your FREE Chains Checklist at www.33yearsaslave.com

Where did these Chains of Unhappiness come from?

_____

_____

_____

_____

_____

_____

_____

What is it costing me to continue to wear these Chains of Unhappiness?

_____

_____

_____

_____

_____

_____

_____

Get your FREE Chains Checklist at www.33yearsaslave.com

DAY 12

The Chains of Debt

Debt is a whole other beast! It is the ultimate mismanagement of money. The ultimate sign of ignoring the responsibility of owing and paying debt. If you cannot handle the little you have, how can you handle the more that you are seeking? This part is going to require being brutally honest with yourself, and working through the challenge of being free from debt.

What Chains of Debt am I wearing?

_____

_____

_____

_____

_____

_____

Where did these Chains of Debt come from?

_____
_____
_____
_____
_____
_____

What is it costing me to continue to wear these Chains of Debt?

_____
_____
_____
_____
_____
_____

Get your FREE Chains Checklist at www.33yearsaslave.com

DAY 13

The Chains of Promotion

Some think that promotions are an indication that you have done well on the job to be rewarded. The reality is that promotion in some businesses depends on who you know, how well you play the political game of doing as you're told, etc. It leaves us chasing the promotion status, rather than chasing our dreams and promoting ourselves.

What Chains of Promotion am I wearing?

_____
_____
_____
_____
_____
_____

Where did these Chains of Promotion come from?

_____
_____
_____
_____
_____
_____

What is it costing me to continue to wear these Chains of Promotion?

_____
_____
_____
_____
_____
_____

Get your FREE Chains Checklist at www.33yearsaslave.com

DAY 14
The Chains of Failure

No one wants to fail! But failure is a part of success. Until you have failed at some things, you wouldn't be able to reach the level of success. It's all about perception. Instead of being stagnated by failure, look at it as an adjustment to get all the pieces to fit together effectively.

What Chains of Failure am I wearing and allowed to keep me stuck?

_____
_____
_____
_____
_____
_____

Where did these Chains of Failure come from?

_____
_____
_____
_____
_____
_____

What is it costing me to continue to wear these Chains of Failure?

_____
_____
_____
_____
_____

Get your FREE Chains Checklist at www.33yearsaslave.com

DAY 15

The Chains of Parenting

While being a parent is an amazing experience, sometimes we spend MORE time and energy investing in our children's dreams than we do our own. As long as we live we owe it to ourselves to not only do for our kids, but to do the best for ourselves so that we set an even better example for our children.

What Chains of Parenting am I wearing?

_____
_____
_____
_____
_____
_____

Get your FREE Chains Checklist at www.33yearsaslave.com

Where did these chains of Parenting come from?

_____

_____

_____

_____

_____

_____

What is it costing me to continue to wear these Chains of Parenting?

_____

_____

_____

_____

_____

_____

Get your FREE Chains Checklist at www.33yearsaslave.com

DAY 16

The Chains of Moving Up the Ladder

I can't tell you how many years I did whatever it took to get a promotion and finally move on up the ladder. Only to STILL be working paycheck to paycheck. I chased promotions instead of promoting myself in my business. It took me too long to realize that as long as I worked for someone else, I would only get a portion of what was due to me.

What Chains of Moving Up the Ladder am I wearing?

_____
_____
_____
_____
_____
_____

Get your FREE Chains Checklist at www.33yearsaslave.com

Where did these Chains of Moving Up the Ladder come from?

_____
_____
_____
_____
_____
_____

What is it costing me to continue to wear these Chains of Moving Up the Ladder?

_____
_____
_____
_____
_____
_____

Get your FREE Chains Checklist at www.33yearsaslave.com

DAY 17
The Chains of Following

When I started to realize what my life had truly become, I realized that not MUCH of my life was what I wanted and that most of my life was MORE of following others. Following others to work, following others to restaurants; more often without a thought as to what my perfect life would look like. When I started to realize that ONLY those chart their own course can truly be happy, I stopped following.

What Chains of Following am I wearing?

_____
_____
_____
_____
_____
_____

Get your FREE Chains Checklist at www.33yearsaslave.com

Where did these Chains of Following come from?

_____

_____

_____

_____

_____

What is it costing me to continue to wear these Chains of Following?

_____

_____

_____

_____

_____

Get your FREE Chains Checklist at www.33yearsaslave.com

DAY 18

The Chains of Being Stuck

'Fight' and 'Flight' are not the only ways we manifest fear. There is also a level call 'Frozen'. At this level we are SO afraid as to what may come that we would rather be consumed by where we are than by moving forward. There were many years that I spent stuck that I wished I would have just gotten the help to move forward.

What Chains of Stuck am I wearing?

_____
_____
_____
_____
_____
_____

Get your FREE Chains Checklist at www.33yearsaslave.com

Where did these Chains of Stuck come from?

___

What is it costing me to continue to wear these Chains of Stuck?

___

Get your FREE Chains Checklist at www.33yearsaslave.com

DAY 19

The Chains of Stagnation

Stagnant water will kill you. And so will a stagnant life. Stagnant water, just like a stagnant life, causes germs to breed because there is no movement. We live in an ever moving world, so it is unnatural for us to sit still.

What Chains of Stagnation am I wearing?

_____
_____
_____
_____
_____
_____

Where did these Chains of Stagnation come from?

_____

_____

_____

_____

_____

_____

What is it costing me to continue to wear these Chains of Stagnation?

_____

_____

_____

_____

_____

_____

Get your FREE Chains Checklist at www.33yearsaslave.com

DAY 20
The Chains of Lies

I think when I started to figure out that I had been LIED to about what made a perfect life, it almost took me out. You see, many people tell you that good jobs, marriages, the perfect house and kids are what make you happy. Lies. The truth is that everyone's happiness looks different because we are all different.

What Chains of Lies am I wearing?

_____

_____

_____

_____

_____

_____

Get your FREE Chains Checklist at www.33yearsaslave.com

Where did these Chains of Lies come from?

_____
_____
_____
_____
_____
_____

What is it costing me to continue to wear these Chains of Lies?

_____
_____
_____
_____
_____
_____

Get your FREE Chains Checklist at www.33yearsaslave.com

DAY 21

The Chains of MORE Education

They say fool me once shame on you… well I was fooled about the promise of more education meaning more money, so much so that I went back to school, racked up more student loans, only to STILL be living paycheck to paycheck. As this world changes, there is a different type of knowledge that we need to possess in order to leave poverty. That is the knowledge of making our own money.

What Chains of MORE education am I wearing?

_____
_____
_____
_____
_____
_____

Where did these Chains of MORE education come from?

_____
_____
_____
_____
_____
_____

What is it costing me to continue to wear these Chains of MORE education?

_____
_____
_____
_____
_____
_____

Get your FREE Chains Checklist at www.33yearsaslave.com

DAY 22

The Chains of the Mind

Our first level of success comes with the mind. We HAVE what we feel we deserve! In my mind, I didn't think I was capable of more, so I didn't have more. I am amazed at how I was limiting myself mentally and how that domino's into me living an unhappy life.

What Chains of Mind am I wearing?

_____
_____
_____
_____
_____
_____

Get your FREE Chains Checklist at www.33yearsaslave.com

Where did these Chains of Minds come from?

_____

_____

_____

_____

_____

_____

What is it costing me to continue to wear these Chains of Mind?

_____

_____

_____

_____

_____

_____

Get your FREE Chains Checklist at www.33yearsaslave.com

DAY 23

The Chains of Life

EVERYONE lives difficult lives. The key is to not allow the trials of life to overwhelm us and wipe us out. We fall down, but the getting up is what is most important. Life is life for everyone, but how we manage our difficulties is what results in our success.

What Chains of Life am I wearing?

_____

_____

_____

_____

_____

_____

Get your FREE Chains Checklist at www.33yearsaslave.com

Where did these Chains of Life come from?

_____
_____
_____
_____
_____
_____

What is it costing me to continue to wear these Chains of Life?

_____
_____
_____
_____
_____
_____

Get your FREE Chains Checklist at www.33yearsaslave.com

DAY 24

The Chains of Ignorance

You don't know what you don't know. That is not the problem. The problem is that we don't SEEK knowledge. We don't SEEK to know more. And with so many books and other forms of education around us, that is a shame. Seek knowledge and ALL will be given unto you.

What Chains of Ignorance am I wearing?

_____
_____
_____
_____
_____
_____

Where did these Chains of Ignorance come from?

_____

_____

_____

_____

_____

_____

What is it costing me to continue to wear these Chains of Ignorance?

_____

_____

_____

_____

_____

_____

Get your FREE Chains Checklist at www.33yearsaslave.com

DAY 25
The Chains of Salary

At it's BEST definition, Salary is a trick. They inflate the amount of money you are receiving but, if you are not careful, they also inflate the amount of hours you are working. So if you ever sit still long enough, you are working for WAY less than what you are supposed to with WAY more job responsibilities than they would ever pay you for. The only way around this is to make your OWN money and create your OWN business.

What Chains of Salary am I wearing?

_____
_____
_____
_____
_____
_____

Get your FREE Chains Checklist at www.33yearsaslave.com

Where did these Chains of Salary come from?

_____
_____
_____
_____
_____
_____

What is it costing me to continue to wear these Chains of Salary?

_____
_____
_____
_____
_____
_____

Get your FREE Chains Checklist at www.33yearsaslave.com

DAY 26

The Chains of Negative Thoughts

Who says WHO can and WHO can't be successful? The truth is that it starts with our own thoughts. When you spend every day thinking of what you can't do, wrapped up in negative thoughts, it is almost impossible to realize what you CAN do. Only once you start to shift your negative thoughts to positive thoughts, and negative people to positive people, do you start to see positive progress.

What Chains of Negative Thoughts am I wearing?

_____
_____
_____
_____
_____
_____

Get your FREE Chains Checklist at www.33yearsaslave.com

Where did these Chains of Negative Thoughts come from?

_____

_____

_____

_____

_____

_____

What is it costing me to continue to wear these Chains of Negative Thoughts?

_____

_____

_____

_____

_____

_____

Get your FREE Chains Checklist at www.33yearsaslave.com

DAY 27

The Chains of Business

I don't know why so many people think they can start a million dollar business without help. You can't. While starting your business is very appealing, you must be willing to invest the same time, energy and effort in starting a business that you invest in a job. There is no such thing as overnight success, the work is hard, but it is all worth it.

What Chains of Business am I wearing?

_____
_____
_____
_____
_____
_____

Where did these Chains of Business come from?

_____
_____
_____
_____
_____
_____

What is it costing me to continue to wear these Chains of Business?

_____
_____
_____
_____
_____
_____

Get your FREE Chains Checklist at www.33yearsaslave.com

DAY 28
The Chains of Deception

I must warn you that there are a LOT of business ventures that will tempt you with the "get rich quick" scheme. They will tell you that working for them will give you that peace of mind of stability. And then they lure you in deeper with that paycheck schedule that shows you when you can expect to be paid regularly. Before you know it, you've settled into being paid the same pay, with increased responsibilities that hide behind the job description "other duties as assigned."

What Chains of Deception am I wearing?

_____

_____

_____

_____

Where did these Chains of Deception come from?

_____
_____
_____
_____
_____
_____

What is it costing me to continue to wear these Chains of Deception

_____
_____
_____
_____
_____
_____

Get your FREE Chains Checklist at www.33yearsaslave.com

DAY 29
The Chains of Time

Time is the GREAT equalizer. No man has more or less time than the other. In order to make the best of our time that we have, time management is imperative. Being intentional about what we do with the time we have.

What Chains of Time am I wearing?

_____
_____
_____
_____
_____
_____

Where did these Chains of Time come from?

_____

_____

_____

_____

_____

_____

What is it costing me to continue to wear these Chains of Time?

_____

_____

_____

_____

_____

_____

Get your FREE Chains Checklist at www.33yearsaslave.com

DAY 30
My Chains

Go back and review what YOUR biggest AH HA's were in this journal. Select the TOP 5 (five) that you want to work on now. Remember you can't boil the ocean, meaning you can't fix everything at once. These chains were not placed on you overnight, and they won't be removed overnight.

My Top 5 Chains

1. _____

2. _____

3. _____

4. _____

5. _____

DAY 31
My Biggest Chain

Breaking chains is a habit. Once you break the biggest chain, then you have more leverage to break the others. What is your BIGGEST chain, and what are some things you can do to break that chain? Keep in mind that ANYTHING can be broken with time and practice.

_____
_____
_____
_____
_____

DAY 32

Removing the Chains

Before you get started, we want to identify some obstacles that you have to removing chains BEFORE they come up. You know in your heart of hearts what they are, so list them below and what you plan on doing to ensure they don't get you caught up in your process.

_____
_____
_____
_____
_____
_____

DAY 33

Free From Chains

Part of being free is that you have to SEE yourself being free. Vision is a HUGE part of breaking chains. Name the TOP 5 things that will be different when you break your chains. Start to visualize and work towards those things daily. Start to look for opportunities to bring those things from your thoughts and into fruition.

1. _____

2. _____

3. _____

4. _____

5. _____

ABOUT THE AUTHOR

Jennifer King is a retired Regional Director for the Texas Department of Criminal Justice who has recrafted her life to help others be FREE to live a life they love.

Serving 33 years in her position being a self-admitted "slave" to what was important to other people, Jennifer now spends her time helping women realize that life is too short NOT to do what you love and that you can profit JUST as well from what you LOVE as you can from building someone else's dreams.

As Regional Director for the Texas Department of Criminal Justice, Jennifer received numerous awards, including the Texas Corrections Associations Star Award.

As an entrepreneur, she has been honored with the New Entrepreneur Expo Award as well as the Influential Black Women in Houston Award, as her work with freeing women takes her all over the country.

Prior to creating the opportunities that would "free" her, Jennifer spent many years in leadership positions with several Multi-Level Marketing companies until she realized that what she had in her hand was enough to set her free.

Both friends and colleagues describe Jennifer as being hardworking and dedicated to the mission while still being focused on FUN!

If you are ready to be FREE from the chains of life that hold you bound, Jennifer is THE expert for you to work with to bridge the gap between your reality and your dreams. After all, she FREED herself so it's likely she can share the tools to FREE you too.

Jennifer resides full time in Austin, Texas and is the mother of two boys, 24 and 12 years old respectively, whom she loves dearly.

Get your FREE Chains Checklist at www.33yearsaslave.com

Made in the USA
Coppell, TX
18 July 2021